M000083553

As you begin to pay attention to your own

stories and what they say about you, you

will enter into the exciting process of becoming,

as you should be, the author of your own

life, the creator of your own possibilities.

MANDY AFTEL

ACKNOWLEDGEMENTS

WITH SPECIAL THANKS TO:
Jason Aldrich, Gerry Baird, Jay Baird, Neil Beaton, Josie Bissett, Laura Boro, Melissa Carlson, M.H. Clark, Tiffany Parente Connors, Jim & Alyssa Darragh & Family, Rob Estes, Pamela Farrington, Michael & Leianne Flynn & Family, Sarah Forster, Miriam Hathaway & Family, Liz Heinlein & Family, Renee & Brad Holmes, Jennifer Hurwitz, Heidi Jones, Sheila Kamuda, Michelle Kim, Carol Anne Kennedy, June Martin, David Miller, Carin Moore & Family, Moose, Jessica Phoenix & Tom DesLongchamp, Janet Potter & Family, Joanna Price, Heidi & Jose Rodriguez, Diane Roger, Alie Satterlee, Kirsten & Garrett Sessions, Emma Sorensen, Andrea Summers, Brien Thompson, Helen Tsao, Anne Whiting, Kobi & Heidi Yamada & Family, Justi and Tote Yamada & Family, Bob & Val Yamada, Kaz & Kristin Yamada & Family, Tai & Joy Yamada, Anne Zadra, August & Arline Zadra, and Gus & Rosie Zadra.

CREDITS

Compiled by Dan Zadra

Designed by Steve Potter

2nd Printing.   Printed in China

GRATITUDE every day.

COMPENDIUM™
INCORPORATED

live inspired.

1/1/19 Gratitude for having the time to read a book in 3 days- "My Oxford Year." So nice to just read! Loved the book, too.

1/5/19 Having a beautiful home ~~to~~ in which to stay warm on this cold winter day.

1/11 Finny for his energy and affection.

All that is worth
cherishing begins
in the heart.

SUZANNE CHAPIN

GRATITUDE every day.

I have a beautiful
blank book and
each night before
I go to bed,
I write down five
things that I can
be grateful about
that day.

SARAH BAN BREATHNACH

GRATITUDE every day.

Today a new sun
rises for me...
everything seems
to speak to me
of my passion,
everything invites
me to cherish it.

ANNE DE LENCLOS

GRATITUDE every day.

Perceive and
rejoice that life
is abundant,
that beauty and
goodness are
amply available...
that happiness is
in your hands.

PAUL HODGES

GRATITUDE every day.

Open your arms
as wide as you can
to receive all the
miracles with your
name on them.

SUZANNA THOMPSON

GRATITUDE every day.

I asked for all
things, that I
might enjoy life.
I was given life,
that I might enjoy
all things.

UNKNOWN

GRATITUDE every day.

As you cherish
the things most
worthwhile in
your family life,
cherish the things
most worthwhile
in your work life.

WILLIAM GIVEN

GRATITUDE every day.

When the sun rises,
I go to work,
When the sun goes
down, I take my rest.
I share creation.
Kings can do no more.

CHINESE VERSE

GRATITUDE every day.

Next to excellence
is the appreciation
of it.

WILLIAM MAKEPEACE
THACKERAY

GRATITUDE every day.

Look for the
good and praise
it. Everyone
appreciates being
appreciated.

BOB MOAWAD

GRATITUDE every day.

Encourage
each other to
become the
best you can
be. Celebrate
what you want
to see more of.

TOM PETERS

GRATITUDE every day.

Appreciation is
a wonderful thing:
it makes what is
excellent in others
belong to us as well.

VOLTAIRE

GRATITUDE every day.

If we're too busy
to enjoy and
appreciate life,
we're too busy.

JEFF DAVIDSON

GRATITUDE every day.

Life is not a
race to be run,
it's a journey
to be savored
every step of
the way.

KOBI YAMADA

GRATITUDE every day.

My heart gives
thanks for empty
moments given to
dreams, and for
thoughtful people
who help those
dreams come true.

WILLIAM S. BRAITHWAITE

GRATITUDE every day.

Thank you to all
those people in my
life who changed
it for the better by
a word, a gift,
an example.

PAM BROWN

GRATITUDE every day.

Good people
increase the
value of every
other person
they influence
in any way.

KELLY ANN ROTHAUS

GRATITUDE every day.

The lives that have
been the greatest
blessing to others
are very often the
lives of those who
themselves were
unaware of having
been a blessing.

OSWALD CHAMBERS

GRATITUDE every day.

Be grateful, truly
grateful, for one
good friend or
thoughtful person.

SHAWNA CORLEY

GRATITUDE every day.

We are so very
rich if we know
just a few people
in a way in which
we know no others.

CATHERINE
BRAMWELL-BOOTH

The best effect of
good people is felt
after we have left
their presence.

RALPH WALDO EMERSON

GRATITUDE every day.

The people you
meet become a
part of you. They
leave their imprints
not just on you,
but inside you.

UNKNOWN

GRATITUDE every day.

There are people
whom one loves
and appreciates
immediately and
forever. Even to
know they are
alive in the world
is quite enough.

NANCY SPAIN

GRATITUDE every day.

Our lives are
filled with simple
joys and blessings
without end;
And one of the
greatest joys in life
is to have a friend.

UNKNOWN

GRATITUDE every day.

My friends
are my estate.

EMILY DICKINSON

GRATITUDE every day.

It is not how much
we appreciate
someone, it is how
much they know it.

ANDREW LYON

GRATITUDE every day.

Say "thank you."
You can't see it
or touch it, but it
goes straight to
the heart.

DAISY SAUNDERS

GRATITUDE every day.

Appreciation can
make a day—even
change a life.

MARGARET COUSINS

GRATITUDE every day.

"Why did you do
all this for me?"
he asked. "I don't
deserve it..."
And Charlotte
replied, "You have
been my friend.
That in itself is a
tremendous thing."

E.B. WHITE

GRATITUDE every day.

It is lovely, when I
forget all birthdays,
including my own,
to find that somebody
remembers me.

ELLEN GLASGOW

GRATITUDE every day.

Send your friends
flowers on normal
days. Send some
to yourself, too,
now and then.
You deserve it.

DON WARD

GRATITUDE every day.

We relish news
of our heroes,
forgetting that we
are extraordinary
to someone too.

HELEN HAYES

GRATITUDE every day.

Among God's
greatest gifts
to us are the
people who
love us.

UNKNOWN

GRATITUDE every day.

Love is a gift.
You can't buy it,
you can't find it,
someone has to
give it to you.

KURT LANGNER

GRATITUDE every day.

One of the
most important
aspects of a
loving relationship
is gratitude to
the other for the
gifts he or she
bestows.

JOAN BORYSENKO, PH.D.

GRATITUDE every day.

It's a compliment
just being born:
to feel, breathe,
think, play, dance,
sing, work, and
make love for this
particular lifetime.

DAPHNE ROSE KINGMA

GRATITUDE every day.

Live your life
while you have it.
Life is a splendid
gift—there is nothing
small about it.

FLORENCE NIGHTINGALE

GRATITUDE every day.

Celebrate your
existence!

WILLIAM BLAKE

GRATITUDE every day.

That I am
here today
is a wonderful
mystery to which
I will respond
with joy.

UNKNOWN

GRATITUDE every day.

Not what we say
about our blessings,
but how we use
them, is the true
measure of our
appreciation.

W.T. PURKISER

GRATITUDE every day.

You have a gift
that only you
can give the
world...The
miracle of your
existence calls
for celebration
every day.

OPRAH WINFREY

GRATITUDE every day.

It came to me
that having life
itself, life being
such a miraculous
achievement, is
like winning the
grand prize.

EARL NIGHTINGALE

GRATITUDE every day.

I love living.
I have some
problems with my
life, but living
is the best thing
they've come up
with so far.

NEIL SIMON

GRATITUDE every day.

No longer forward
nor behind I look
in hope or fear;
But, grateful, take
the good I find,
The best of now
and here.

JOHN GREENLEAF
WHITTIER

GRATITUDE every day.

For everything you
have missed in life,
you have gained
something else.

RALPH WALDO EMERSON

GRATITUDE every day.

Thanks for showing
me that even on the
darkest, rainiest
days the sun is still
there, just behind
the clouds, waiting
to shine again.

LISA HARLOW

GRATITUDE every day.

May you never
miss a sunset or a
rainbow because you
are looking down.

SARA JUNE PARKER

GRATITUDE every day.

Life does not have
to be perfect to be
wonderful.

ANNETTE FUNICELLO

GRATITUDE every day.

Life, even in the
hardest times, is
full of moments
to savor. They will
not come this
way again, not
in this way.

PAULA RINEHART

GRATITUDE every day.

We can stop
waiting for life
to become perfect
and start working
with what we've
got...We can accept,
bless, give thanks,
and get going.

SARAH BAN BREATHNACH

GRATITUDE every day.

Think of all the
ills from which
you are exempt.

JOSEPH JOUBERT

GRATITUDE every day.

Difficult times
have helped me to
understand better
than before how
infinitely rich and
beautiful life is in
every way...

ISAK DINESEN

GRATITUDE every day.

More stuff
doesn't make
people happier.

BILL McKIBBEN

GRATITUDE every day.

How many are
the things I can
do without!

SOCRATES

GRATITUDE every day.

If you want to
feel rich, just
count all the
gifts you have
that money
cannot buy.

PROVERB

GRATITUDE every day.

Not what we have,
but what we enjoy,
constitutes our
abundance.

JOHN PETIT-SENN

GRATITUDE every day.

If you're honest
about it, and
you count all
your assets,
you always
show a profit.

ROBERT QUILLEN

GRATITUDE every day.

I was rich, if not
in money, in sunny
hours and summer
days, and spent
them lavishly.

HENRY DAVID THOREAU

GRATITUDE every day.

Practice expanding
your capacity to be
delighted.

UNKNOWN

GRATITUDE every day.

I was in love with
the whole world
and all that lived
in its rainy arms.

LOUISE ERDRICH

GRATITUDE every day.

The cream of
enjoyment in this
life is always
impromptu. The
chance walk; the
unexpected visit;
the unpremeditated
journey...

FANNY FERN

GRATITUDE every day.

To look at
everything
always as
though you
were seeing it
either for the
first or last time:
Thus is your
time on earth
filled with glory.

BETTY SMITH

GRATITUDE every day.

I took a walk on
Spaulding's farm
the other afternoon.
I saw the setting
sun lighting up the
opposite side of a
stately pine wood.

HENRY DAVID THOREAU

GRATITUDE every day.

The sun does not
shine for a few
trees and flowers,
but for the wide
world's joy,
including yours.

HENRY WARD BEECHER

GRATITUDE every day.

Stop every now
and then. Just stop
and enjoy. Take a
deep breath. Relax
and take in the
abundance of life.

UNKNOWN

GRATITUDE every day.

The day, water,
sun, moon, night—
I do not have to
purchase these
things with money.

PLAUTUS

GRATITUDE every day.

It's difficult to
think anything but
pleasant thoughts
while eating
a home-grown
tomato.

LEWIS GRIZZARD

GRATITUDE every day.

If you wish to know
the divine, feel the
wind on your face
and the warm sun
on your hand.

BUDDHA

The best things in
life are nearest:
Breath in your
nostrils, light in
your eyes, flowers
at your feet, duties
at your hand...

ROBERT LOUIS STEVENSON

GRATITUDE every day.

Make the most
of every sense;
glory in all of
the pleasures and
beauty which the
world reveals to
you...

HELEN KELLER

GRATITUDE every day.

There are moments...
when I feel a deep
gratitude, when I sit
at the open window
and there is a blue
sky or moving clouds.

KÄTHE KOLLWITZ

GRATITUDE every day.

The capacity for
delight is the gift of
paying attention.

JULIE CAMERON

GRATITUDE every day.

There are flowers
everywhere, for
those who bother
to look.

HENRI MATISSE

GRATITUDE every day.

The sunrise, of
course, doesn't
care if we watch
it or not. It will
keep on being
beautiful, even if
no one bothers
to look at it.

GENE AMOLE

GRATITUDE every day.

While pursuing all
you want, be sure
to appreciate and
enjoy all you have.

JIM ROHN

GRATITUDE every day.

Remember
that what you
now have was
once among
the things only
hoped for.

EPICURUS

GRATITUDE every day.

All the great
blessings of
my life are
present in my
thoughts today.

PHOEBE CARY

GRATITUDE every day.

See, the good
is lying here.
Seize it with a
bold endeavor,
Happiness is
always near.

JOHANN WOLFGANG
VON GOETHE

Life is a child
playing around
your feet, a tool
you hold firmly in
your grip, a bench
you sit down upon
in the evening, in
your garden.

JEAN ANOUILH

GRATITUDE every day.

Appreciation of life
itself, becoming
suddenly aware
of the miracle of
being alive, on
this planet, can
turn what we call
ordinary life into
a miracle.

DAN WAKEFIELD

GRATITUDE every day.

The moments of
happiness we
enjoy take us by
surprise. It is
not that we seize
them, but that
they seize us.

ASHLEY MONTAGU

GRATITUDE every day.

Take spring when
it comes, and
rejoice. Take
happiness when
it comes, and
rejoice. Take love
when it comes,
and rejoice.

CARL EWALD

GRATITUDE every day.

There are two
kinds of gratitude:
The sudden kind
we feel for what
we take, the larger
kind we feel for
what we give.

EDWIN ROBINSON

GRATITUDE every day.

We tire of those
pleasures we take,
but never of those
we give.

JOHN PETIT-SENN

GRATITUDE every day.

Thank you to all
the people in the
world who are
always ten percent
kinder than they
need to be.

HELEN EXLEY

GRATITUDE every day.

Be thankful
when you're
tired and weary
because it
means you've
probably made
a difference in
someone's life
today.

UNKNOWN

GRATITUDE every day.

I am learning
what it means to
be grateful. The
more I think, the
more I thank.

UNKNOWN

GRATITUDE every day.

We are misled from
early childhood
to think that life
is something you
get through. Life is
something to be in.

DUSTIN HOFFMAN

GRATITUDE every day.

We have not been
sufficiently schooled
in the moment.

STREPHON KAPLAN-WILLIAMS

GRATITUDE every day.

I say to the
moment: Stay
now! You are
so beautiful!

JOHANN WOLFGANG
VON GOETHE

GRATITUDE every day.

Life is a highway,
but I've tossed my
maps and GPS.
If something neat
turns up along the
way, I am stopping
to take pictures.

MATTHEW WOLFE

GRATITUDE every day.

When life gives
you a detour, enjoy
and appreciate the
scenery.

MICHAEL NOLAN

GRATITUDE every day.

Everything is a
once-in-a-lifetime
experience.

KOBI YAMADA

GRATITUDE every day.

With each new day
I put away the past
and discover the
new beginnings I
have been given.

ANGELA L. WOZNIAK

GRATITUDE every day.

Normal day, let
me be aware of
the treasure you
are. Let me learn
from you, love you,
bless you before
you depart.

MARY JEAN IRION

GRATITUDE every day.

Some blessings—
like rainbows after
rain or a friend's
listening ear—
are extraordinary
gifts waiting to be
discovered in an
ordinary day.

UNKNOWN

GRATITUDE every day.

Think of a special
ordinary occasion
(the sunset? the
presence of one
you care for?)
and how you can
celebrate it today.

DAVID KUNDTZ

GRATITUDE every day.

In order to be
utterly happy
the only thing
necessary is
to refrain from
comparing this
moment with other
moments in the
past...or future.

ANDRÉ GIDE

GRATITUDE every day.

Every day is
my best day;
this is my life;
I'm not going
to have this
moment again.

BERNIE SIEGEL

GRATITUDE every day.

I always say to
myself, what is
the most important
thing I can think
about at this
extraordinary
moment?

BUCKMINSTER FULLER

GRATITUDE every day.

Memories
are perhaps
the greatest
gifts of all.

GLORIA GAITHER

GRATITUDE every day.

My diaries were
written primarily,
I think, not to
preserve the
experience but
to savor it...

ANNE MORROW
LINDBERGH

GRATITUDE every day.

What a wonderful
life I've had. I only
wish I'd realized
it sooner.

COLETTE

Time is a very
precious gift—
so precious that
it is only given
to us moment by
moment.

AMELIA BARR

GRATITUDE every day.

Never squander
an opportunity to
tell someone you
love or appreciate
them.

KELLY ANN ROTHAUS

GRATITUDE every day.

Treasure each other
in the recognition
that we do not know
how long we shall
have each other.

JOSHUA LOTH LIEBMAN

GRATITUDE every day.

Each day is a new
life. Seize, live,
love and cherish it.

KAREN POWELL

GRATITUDE every day.

Each birthday
will be a gift of
time, and growing
old will be a gift
of life.

UNKNOWN

GRATITUDE every day.

See golden
days, fruitful of
golden deeds,
with joy and love
triumphing.

JOHN MILTON

GRATITUDE every day.

Evermore thanks.

WILLIAM SHAKESPEARE

GRATITUDE every day.